WHEN
HEARTS
RUN ON
BATTERIES

BOOKS BY XYVAH OKOYE

The God-Seeker Collection
Thy Will Be Done
Understanding Christianity
Chasing God
Show Me Your Glory
Why Christians go to Church

Events To Emotions Collection
A Darker Shade of Light
When Hearts Run on Batteries

EVENTS TO EMOTIONS

Xyvah Okoye

WHEN HEARTS RUN ON BATTERIES

WHEN HEARTS RUN ON BATTERIES

Paperback ISBN: 978-1-915129-03-1

Published by Chartus.X
First published in 2019 by the author
This edition published in 2022

Copyright ©Xyvah Okoye, 2019

To all those dealing with things
they don't talk about.

CONTENTS

ALWAYS FOREVER

When love is lost and hope ends,
And the tragedy sends volts of pain from your
heart to your brain, incapacitating you
That's when you know your heart is broken.

When the million words can't bind the million
pieces you can't seem to find as your cardia
erupted,
Volcanic regret like lava leaking down your soul
till time leaves only ashes cocooned by loss.

So, the sun smites you not by day nor the moon
by night because you retreat to inhabit a steel
house made of four plain walls that will not be
blown down by empty promises and false
declarations of "Forever Love."

Too scared to let in the light that once led you
to the lover who tore your world apart when
you still believed in having a heart…
In love…
In hope…
Hoping against hope that, against all odds, you'll
defeat the enemy battling for your soul, all the
while wondering what profit it would be to give
it all up and gain the world
After all, all that's left is ashes
But from ashes to ashes, from dust to flames,
like a Phoenix you rise again to laugh, to love, to
cry.

And though you feel the ache inside, you hide
the pain behind vodka and sex games.
Too ashamed to admit to yourself that you got
played, you master the game, enslaving the
world as the world became your playing ground
and power became the aim,
You became a slave to your senses
All in a bid to avoid the pain of a broken heart.

But back to the start
To the one with the broken heart and the burnt-out soul.
To the one who almost lost their mind when the enemy stole the little hope in the heart that lit up the part of life that ever meant anything.
To the one step forward, three steps back
Stepping on glass like steppingstones, wanting to feel pain—
No! To feel…
Alone knowing all along that it isn't the "Forever Love" lost forever that causes the worst pain…
It's the now in the "always forever" that never came.

BEAUTIFULLY BROKEN

Raindrops dripping down the window,
mirroring the tears running down her cheek,
A race down gravity lane, with no winner and all
none the wiser, as the pieces of her broken heart
hit the ground in first place.

Tears like blood outline the smile spread sweetly
across her pained face
As she begins to comprehend the beauty behind
the brokenness,
the bliss beyond the pain.

The loss hurt, but the love was worth it
And now, learning to let go, she smiles with
gratitude for the broken-hearted girl reflected in
the window.

Because, although the raindrops caress her oblivious reflection, she is aware of the truth: She may have lost a lover, but she never lost love.

Between Two Worlds

Trapped between two worlds…
I cannot go forward
But I cannot go back to who I've been

The path ahead is broad and inviting
I need only take one step
And I'm carried all the way
The path behind, the straight and narrow
Holds trails of my blood, dripping
As I have walked it all this time.

The path set before me, the one I need take,
Is the path I am supposed to have left behind.
The path left behind me, the one I must take,
Is the path I am supposed to leave behind

"Never look back! Never go back!"
I learnt on the path I now leave behind,

So how then, am I to go back?
To look back at what was?
To follow again the straight and narrow,
When it's the path I leave behind?

I'm still pressing on the upward way
And my way has led me here.
Do I walk on forward to the broad-way future?
Or do I turn back? Retreat? Surrender?
Retrace my blood trailed steps
To live out my future in the past?

I am trapped between two worlds…
I cannot go forward
But I cannot go back to who I've been.

CAMOUFLAGE MY THOUGHTS

I hear the bombs exploding,
The screams of men and women around me,
The unfortunate lives ended by one wrong step.

Arms and legs blown off
After all, if your arm causes you to sin…
And then again,
The screams grow louder, the fire burns, the
smell of blood and burning flesh fills my lungs,
I need to escape.

No one can
rescue me.
I need freedom
from the catastrophe
around me.
So, I open my eyes,

Drown my senses with a mix of one part vodka and two parts pills,
Hoping it will be enough to distract me from the war going on inside my head.

CIRCLE OF LIFE

All reactions are to actions
And all actions cause reactions
All words can build or break
All wounds can mend or make

All friends have something in common
And being uncommon is something in common
All people tend to make friends
And all friends tend to make people

All pains cause a hurt
And all hurts cause pain
All wounds may let out blood
And all blood lets out remains

Every sound breaks a silence
Every silence too, breaks a sound

And every song comes from the heart
As the heart is inspired in every song

The fun in life is made by you
And so also, the fun makes you
The wrong always has something right
So as there is always wrong in right.

The master mostly teaches the pupil
But it's the pupil who teaches him to teach
The lawyer does defend his client
But the client has to defend him too

There's a law that pulls things down
That same law makes things go round
If you roll a boulder from Chicago
It will come back to Chicago

A circle has no beginning or end
For the beginning is the end
Our human nature and natures miracle
Shows us truly that life is a circle.

CRIMSON TEARS

As beads of blood bleeding red run down my
arm,
The arm of flesh has failed me once again.

And once again I am left alone
Alone with my thoughts, contemplating the
complexities of a simple word… No.

Knowing that the truth was all a lie, I lie here
listening to the sound of my own hearts
arrhythmical beating as the blood it pumps
pours out through emotional gashes across my
left breast.

Gashes that only I can see and feel, invisible
enough to conceal with a smile
So, I smile.

Even when it hurts, I smile.
Even when I can't breathe, I smile.
Even when my world is falling apart, I smile.
Even as the life drains from my body, I smile.

Because a simple smile conceals the myriad of emotions which flood me,
Like the calm sea with its deadly undercurrents,
I am currently drowning in my own pain, with no lifeline or rescue boat. So, I smile.
Knowing that the only escape to my predicament is a permanent solution.
And though some may think it's a temporary problem…

"…The sea is calm today…"
The sea is never calm
She just looks calm sometimes
Her raging currents can wreck ships and drown men
But she knows that, as terrifying as she may be,

People are always attracted to a smile.
And so, she smiles

Beckoning both the simpleton and the
adventurer to come unto her
Welcoming them with open arms
Leading them to believe that the turmoil they
once saw was a temporary problem…
But be not deceived
Like the raging sea, I smile.

And as I lie here staring at the beads of Blood
like crimson tears running down my arm
I realize that it would have been okay to cry
sometimes.

CROSSFIRE

Love is like a bed of roses
Even roses have their thorns
But I can't breathe without you
And even though time proposes
That I forget you and move on
I just can't breathe without you
We fight then we break up
We kiss and we make up
Is this going to be the life that I lead?
Would I cry? Would I bleed?
Would I let my children ever see?

Shotgun fires
I hear voices screaming,
Coming from downstairs
I'm behind the door.
I scan the room and look for shelter

As the bombs begin exploding in my head
Laying on the floor
Somehow, I've been damaged in the crossfire.

Love is not a bed of roses
As every rose must have its thorn
I'll learn to breathe without you
And even as time proposes,
I will forget you and move on
And learn to breathe without you
We fight then we break up
No kiss and no make up
This will never be the life that I lead
I won't cry, I won't bleed
or let my children become me

Shotgun fires
I hear voices screaming,
Coming from downstairs
I'm behind the door.
I scan the room and look for shelter
As the bombs begin exploding in my head

Laying on the floor
Somehow, I've been damaged in the crossfire.

DEAR PAIN

Dear Pain,
My old familiar friend
Despite the hunger and thirst for your company
I have decided to let you go
I have decided to move on
To get on with my life.
It's not like I don't want you anymore
You've been a faithful friend
Sticking closer than a brother
You've been there for me
Through the hard times
through the lonely nights
And the tears flooding my pillow
You've stood by me
Stuck with me
Seen me through it all
I feel like a traitor

For you've been my only true friend
But I know, where I go, you cannot come
And where you are, I cannot remain
So, we will have to go our own separate ways.

FORGET ME NOT

Time changes, things change, people change
As we all head off in our different directions,
I lay at your feet
My one, final, and only request...
Forget me not.

Forget me not as you go along your
way
As the places change and
the strange faces become
familiar.
As the things we once did
become history
And the life we once lived
become a memory.
Please, forget me not.

Forget me not as you go along your way
As the pressures of life begin to weigh heavy on
your shoulders
And the things that brought you joy are far
And the time you have is well spent on surviving
Please, forget me not.

Forget me not as you go along your way
And the distance shreds my heart, tearing us
apart.
Your face remains etched in my brain
As though the first thing I saw this morning
Please, forget me not.

Forget me not as you go along your way
And the healer called time cannot seem to mend
my broken heart
As you hold me in your arms all night
Waking up to the bitter reality of your absence
Please, forget me not.

Don't forget the time we spent

The laughs we had
The love we shared.
I know I can't compare
To what she is to you
But if what we had was ever true
Please, forget me not ... I beg of you.

GRACE I NEED

To believe your word is true
And to believe Lord, there is nothing you can't
do
To believe you're on my side
And to believe that through the storms,
You will hide me in your arms

And give me faith to believe and the courage to
receive the grace I need
Your grace I need
Give me hope to confess your will and nothing
less than grace I need
Your grace I need

Give me courage to confess
That you want the best for me and nothing less
Help me see your will is better than my plans

Help me understand the things you do and open up my fisted hands.

HIS LUXURY COUPÉ

Drunk on my sorrow, high on my pain
With so much to lose and still nothing to gain
Yet I drown in the chaos I call my life
Still believing the man who practically destroyed
my life;

Who took a knife to
my heart, daggered me
with words,
With songs of love, of the birds and the bees
I didn't see beyond the signs, didn't read
between the lines
The truth written in plain ink, though he refused
to sign

I made it my mission, made him my world
Between walks in the park and kisses in the dark
From gazing at the stars so late into the night

He built castles in my head and a moat around
my heart
He locked me in a tower and promised I was his
His good girl, he said, his special little girl
A friend he would never want to lose, he said
The one he wanted to be with, he said
The one who made him happy, he said
Yes, he said, no, he said, please, he said, I'm not
letting you go, he said

No, he said, yes, she said, why, he said, no, she
said, yes, he said
Roles reversed, down in the sheets, the bed
soaked wet,
I bet you didn't expect that, he said
No, she chuckled.
Did you like that? He said, yes, she said
But it hurt, she said... But she didn't say, it hurt

It hurt like daggers pierced through her heart,
Like acid poured on her soul

To know she had been used, and abused by the
love of her life
To know she would never again feel complete
Never again feel whole
For she had given herself away
To someone who would never treasure her
Someone who would never love her

Someone whose heart was made of ice
Whose soul was carved from wood
Whose will was forged in steel
Who had used her to satisfy his raging desires
And held nothing but contempt for her now he
was through.

His luxury coupe, he called her
Now, the other girl, was her name
The face he once loved to hold, to kiss, to
stroke,
He now looked at with hate and disdain
And then she asked herself, why go on?

Why go on living? She gave him her love, gave
him her all
And now she's nothing but an empty shell,

So, she drinks up her sorrows, and rolls up her
pain
She lights it with her future and watches it all
burn
As she drowns herself in a pool of blood
Bleeding from her broken heart.

I AM SPENT

I'm spent.
I don't know how, I don't know why
I don't know where, I don't know when
I just know that I'm spent.

Pouring out my precious ointment
Washing the feet of the one that I love
The one that has no love in his heart for me
I'm spent

Washing his feet with all that's within me
He disregards the tears I cry, my crowning glory,
I lay as a rag to wipe his feet dry
I'm spent

Sitting at his feet to entreat his wisdom
He broods over Martha and her selfish matters
Though I give up my time to be in his presence

I'm spent

My energy poured out as I run to the garden
Still seeking him, though now a lifeless body,
He longs for the ones that mean more to him
than me
I am spent.

Spent my body, that he may adore
Spent my mind to give him more
Spent my heart out on the floor
I am left with nothing more

All for love, I'm spent and sore
Once a prize, of glory, of awe
I now lay empty, lost, and spent
I am spent...

I am no more.

I CRY

I cry
Not for pain or sorrow
Not for grief or loss, I cry
Not for the shattering feeling of love lost,
But for the emptiness of forgetting the feeling
of having ever loved.
For the desperate plea that wells up in my heart,
The incessant longing for feeling, for
sensitivity...
For connection.

I cry because I'm one man on an island,
stranded and left for dead
Forgotten by all, and all for the lack of
connection.
I'm trapped in a cycle of drinks, drugs, and bad
decisions

But don't judge until you've tasted from my
cup...
After all, water and spirits look alike from a
spectator's point of view.

I know I'm making the wrong choices
I know there's a right way to go,
And I know that I'm not going that way.
All for the albatross tied around my neck,
Dragging me clumsily down to hell
But what can I do, when I have nothing left of
my lifeline but a broken piece of string?

And what I wouldn't give to feel connected
again, to one person or another, no matter the
cost,
For I'd rather live my life with the pain of regret,
knowing I loved and lost,
Than live out the rest of my days as numb as a
lamp pole in deep winter.
I'd rather the pain of the cold than the
numbness and lifelessness of no connection...

I'm not tired of being alive, I'm just tired of living without living, but I find comfort in the knowledge that the fight will soon be over, and I'll be able to finally rest in peace.

And as I prepare for my grave, I'm grateful for everything I've learnt and everyone I've met, I'm mostly glad that I'll finally be able to forget.

I HAVE BEEN DECEIVED

I have been deceived
I shan't believe the lies
I shan't believe the tales
I shan't believe it
The bull-crap that comes out of your mouth
The meaningless declarations of love
The false proclamations of affection

I have been deceived
I shan't ignore the truth
I shan't ignore the facts
I shan't ignore the reality
Of who I truly am to you
Of what I truly mean to
you
Of where I truly belong
in your heart

I have been deceived
I can't do this anymore
I can't take it anymore
I don't think I can survive this
I'd much rather believe the lies
Than face it and accept the truth
I really wish the lies were true

I have been deceived
I won't forget the memories
I won't forget the smiles
I won't forget the feeling
Of your lips pressed against mine
Of your body pressed against mine
Of your hands all over my body

I have been deceived
I can't let you go
I shan't let you go
I won't let you go
Though I refuse to believe the lies

Though I decide to accept the truth
I know I won't survive if I let you go.

I WISH

I wish I was filthy rich
I wish I was popular
I wish I was loved
I wish I had true friends

I wish my family loved me
For once, maybe they could understand
The pain I go through
Maybe they could help me
Maybe they could care

I wish I had a real friend
Someone to count on
To share my problems with
Someone to always help me
And talk away those lonely days

I wish a was brilliant
Though I know I already am
I wish I had more than that
To take me places
And make me someone now

I wish that I was rich
There, living my fantasy
Away from the real world
To a place of peace
To some sort of solitude

I wish you were still alive
You didn't have to die
At least, not now at least
You didn't need to go so soon
But trust, God has his reasons

I wish my life was better
Not as miserable as it is
I wish I had real friends like you
Not being me would be great

I would be free from the pain

I wish the world would stop turning
And people would have a heart
I wish that life would be good
That pain wasn't all I felt
And that, for once, people would show love

I wish I knew what it felt like to care
And how it felt to be cared for
And what it meant to love or be loved
And not hate or spite or regret
Or the hardest parts of life

I wish I were dead
Sometimes, maybe all the time
I wish I was away from this life
This life of misery and sorrow and hurt
This lugubrious state called life

I wish I was in heaven
In a state of grace and peace

Though, most times I don't deserve it
I just wish I could go there
To get away from the pain and heartbreak.

IF LOVE IS A CRIME

This funny feeling, I feel when I'm around you
Is unnatural to me
It is very strange to me

Sometimes I think I'm in love
Sometimes I'm not sure
Sometimes I want to be with you
Sometimes I'm scared to do so

If I'm in love with you
Then why is it so strange
Why do I feel so insecure
When I hear or speak your name?

Maybe it's wrong to fall in love
Or should I call it that
Does love really leave you so lost and perplexed
Or does it just help mesmerize?

Well, if this feeling is love
And this feeling is wrong
Then the feeling must be a real crime

Well, if love is a crime
Then I'm a fugitive of the law
For this feeling is lifelong.

I'M LEARNING TO LOVE.

As the wind blew softly, caressing my face, I
realized how much I desired that soft touch. Just
to feel wanted, just to feel needed, just to feel
loved.

So, I'm learning to cherish the feel of the wind,
the soft droplets of cool rain that stroke my hair,
the warm rays of sunshine that kiss my lips.

I'm learning to cherish the sweet smell of freshly
mown lawns and the look of
fallen autumn leaves and,
instead of letting them
remind me of loved ones
and good times, I'm learning
to love these things.

The next caress upon my skin, the next kiss upon my lips, the next gentle, beautiful words whispered into my ear, they will remind me of the love and care nature has shown me, asking for nothing in return.

No catches, no clauses, just pure giving, pure loving which asks not even for my heart, but for me to be happy.

I'm learning to love the things that truly love me.

I'M FINE

I can't begin to count the number of times I've
said "I'm fine"
"I'm alright"
When I'm clearly not.
But sometimes, it's harder to open up and let it
out than to bottle it up and keep it in,
So I choose the easy way out, which is in
And in that moment realize that all I'll ever be is
alone.
I feel tired

I feel tired
Like I want to sleep and not wake up
Like I want to fall from the 75th story
Just fall
I feel like I want to dangle from the tallest tree
with the weight of my heart, head and gravity
helping the noose break my neck

I feel tired of thinking
Tired of breathing
Tired of being
I just want to disappear
To slowly fade away
To cease to exist
And I just feel tired
Tired of each sunrise and sunset ushering in a
new cycle of 24s giving me 24 more reasons to
die before 30
Tired of the sounds of the birds and the bees
and the smell and feel of fresh air and warm sun
on my skin
Cos all I feel is cold, bitter,
empty tiredness

And yet I feel fine, cos fine
means I'm still alive
Still awake
Still hoping to
Still wanting to
And yet not asleep

So, I'm fine

JUST A FACT

Life is painful
Being alive hurts
Breathing is a strenuous exercise
Thinking is an overly complicated process.
Sometimes I think it might be better to just end
it all
And even that feels like more of a struggle than
it's worth.
It's not a complaint, just a fact:
I'm tired of living.
My heart feels tired of beating
My lungs feel tired of breathing
My brain feels tired of thinking
My soul feels tired of feeling
And yet... I go on
Because feeling tired isn't a good enough reason
to quit...
Though it's the best reason I've got... for now...

And so often I fear, if I were to find a better
reason to quit, would I still keep living this life?
Even though my lungs beg for their last breath,
would I still fight for one more?
Would I desire death? Or would I just carry on
not wanting to be alive?

MAYBE

Definitely, heartbreak isn't new
The solution is as painful as the cause
The thought of you makes me confused
Seriously confused

You know, if I had a choice,
I won't be the way I am right now.
You've made the difference in my life
So why do you get scared of me?

I watch the others follow you
You lead them like sheep follow shepherd
I want to be different
But I wish to be part of the flock

I know it's not possible
But if only you knew the way I felt

If only you understood what I was going
through
If only you could see

Then maybe you won't be so adamant
Maybe you'd give me a chance
Maybe you'd help me as a true friend
Maybe you'd feel the same way too.

MUMBO JUMBO

If we never had earth
Then we'd never have flown
If we did not have day
Then our dark times wouldn't be night

If we did not have the sound
We would not hear the silence
And if we did not have the dark
We would not see the light

If we did not live on land
Then we would not go swimming
If we did not grow our hair
Then it wouldn't need trimming

If we do not sit, we cannot stand
And if we do not sand, we cannot sit

If we do not sleep, we cannot awaken
And if we do not awaken, we cannot sleep

All these are done
For the benefit of each other
So should we work together
To help one another

If you love someone, let them know
If they know, they may love you back
Look out for those who love you
And once you know them, love them back

I'm not sure of what I'm saying
And I'm not sure if it's making sense
But the sense brings fun to stupidity
And the stupidity brings fun to the sense

SOMEDAYS

Some days I sit and wish it will all come true
But if you don't get what you want,
What can you do?
A friend was my one wish, something I dreamt
I took it as a prophecy, one that I almost felt

It breaks my heart to know my misconception
of this youth
And once again, I am obliged to believe the
bitter truth

 That friend was not the
real friend
But better
with one
than none

Oh! The pain and all the anger I felt
When that one was gone

I just found out that if I want one, then I have
to be of one's kind
So if you can't accept me for who I really am,
then never mind.

POETRY IN MOTION

As I watch the beads of blood like sweat drip
down my arms
I feel the pressure release
The end is near
This time, I do not hesitate.
My precision is on point, my tension steady
I press down hard and get ready to go.

The aim wasn't to die
It was to cease to exist
And even that, I couldn't do.

PUZZLING QUESTIONS OF THE HEART

Why do people feel pain?
What do they cry over a broken heart?
When they know it cannot be healed?
Why can't others feel your pain
Even when you try your best to express it?

Why do you ask and give but never receive?
Why don't you get what you want?
What do you do when you have to stand and
watch all you've ever wanted given to someone
who never wanted them?

What do you do when you give your heart
To someone who takes it and breaks it?
What do you do when you love everyone
And everyone loved everyone

Everyone except you?

What do you do when you find a friend?
Who builds up your hopes just to bring them
crashing down again?
What do you do when the only one you love?
Is the only one who doesn't love you?

What do you do
When the only one who
Can stop you from crying
Is the one who made you cry?
Puzzling questions of the heart

SCARS

As steady as a beating drum, my heart beats in
my chest...
Pumping blood rushing through my veins to the
tips of my fingers and toes
And only God knows how hard it hurts to stay
alive sometimes...
And when all is said and done, and everyone is
gone,
I'm left alone to dance to the rhythm of my
heart playing in my chest,
And I begin to move, mixing my salsa with my
tears as I gasp for the breath of life for what I
think could be my last time...
And as my head begins to sink, and as my
eyelids slowly shut,
My gaze falls upon my chest...
And I see them...

Those scars...
Those scars I wear across my chest
From times I failed to be the best I could be,
From times people looked and couldn't see any
good in me...
And they threw me aside as they took out the
trash when they were spring cleaning out their
lives...
Scars from times I loved so deep it carved a hole
straight through my heart,
And it took days, and weeks, and months of
surgery,
Lying under the blade of the Word setting
asunder the cause of the incessant bleeding, as
my heart beat faster,
A cupid's arrow lodged in my left auricle
Filling my veins with the poison I called love...
And it was killing me softly...
"I honestly didn't know where to turn
Because everyone I went to seemed to think that
The only problem with my situation was me.

And as the daggers of "encouragement" pierced
through my abdomen,
I realized it was harder to digest the truth
When the rest of the world thought you were
the lie,
And lying there waiting for a Good Samaritan to
hear my silent screams and help me to an inn,
Then I began to realize,
"nobody knows who I really am..."
"Nobody can recognize me..."
"Nobody knows my name."

But somebody did...
And He picked me up...
And He cleaned me up...
And He called me by name...
Not liar, or misfit... He knew my name.
And His voice was sweet as the nectar and
smooth as honey...
And His hands were warm and gentle as he
washed me clean with the water of His Word...
And his touch was so tender,

I didn't even feel the needle stitching me back together again...

And in His eyes was the beauty of sunrise and sunset,

Setting my fractures and mending my wounds

And by the time He was through, they were nothing but scars...

Those scars...

And I said, "Jesus, if you would heal me, Why leave the scars? They only remind me of the hurt..."

I didn't understand then, you see...

Those scars...

The ones He left behind were not only to remind me of the hurt...

They were to remind me of the pain

And the times I hurt so bad

And the loneliness

And the anger

And the loss

And the rejection

And the times I was misunderstood...

And the people I trusted to be for me
Who went before me to hail me as the queen of
the sinners and the condemned...
And I still hear their taunts...
And the names...
And I remember the feel of the earth as I lay
dying,
With smoke in my eyes,
And the smell of the dust filling my lungs and
the taste of my own blood in my mouth...
And you may wonder why I wear them so
proudly...
And you remember me by the scars you gave
me,
By the names you called me...
Like liar and loser, and weak and dysfunctional,
disobedient, a prostitute, disloyal, fake,
unreliable, emotional...
And you look at them and see only flaws
That do not meet your standard of perfection...
Because they symbolize the hardships...
And failures and all the imperfections I embody.

These scars...
And as my shutting eyes fall upon these scars...
I feel it all again... And then I remember...
These scars are the trophies I carry from my battles.
They are the proof that I am more than a conqueror.
And you too will one day recognize me by the scars you have me,
Because they remind me not only of what I've been through...
They remind me that I survived.

<u>SELFISH</u>

When all is said and has been done
What's done is done,
And now begun to go then, when now was
when we had we...
Now me...
No longer us but I
Not you but my once upon a time
Happily ever after singing
"... us against the world, you and me against
them all..."
But when all is said and done
I see it's really the world against just me
Only me
But it's not only about me, I guess, that makes
me selfish, protecting my heart
Which I offered up to you, body and soul and
found lying on the gravel covered floor.

STEP BY STEP

Step by step, we make our way, step by step
A child learns to walk
We all learn to talk
And to grow up like a tree
Sprouting from its seeds

Life is a path, it is a struggle
We make our way through
We push forward,
To grow, to learn, to lead
We try hard to learn to climb

To climb that mountain
To swim that sea
To walk that valley
To cross that desert
To reach the top

We struggle through life
We go through pain
Cross over hurdles
Endure certain sufferings
To make our way

Life is hard
I speak from experience
I wish it all to end
But I know I will make it someday
Step by step, I will make my
way

Step by step

THE REMEDY

Juice dripping down my chin, I swallow a
mouthful of sin
Its fruit, pleasing to my eyes. Its fruit, good for
food
Its fruit, tasting so sweet in my mouth
As it slowly sinks down my throat and into my
belly

I only took a bite, but just one bite was enough
I could feel the poison seeping into my system
Already filling my bloodstream with a slow,
painful death
As it slowly sinks down my throat into my belly

One kiss, one touch, one night was enough
In a moment of weakness, in a turmoil of sheets
Resting in the strong arms of my *savior*

I traded my salvation for one bite of security

Not a fruit, or a tree... One bite of safety
Safety from my loneliness, safety from my
insecurity
From the internal conflict of not being enough
Not slim enough, not smart enough, not good
enough,

Not good enough for someone to want me
Not good enough for someone to love me
Not good enough for someone to choose me
Not good enough for someone to marry me

Me? not me, never me... What about me?
What was wrong with me? What had happened
to me?
Why did it always have to be me?
Why did it always have to be about me?

With my eyes fixed only on me,
blurred hyper-myopia led me to find me a savior

A knight in shining armor who would save me
from me
I needed a hero, not some cross-hung,
tombstone-rolling superstition

All I needed was one bite. Not a tree or a fruit
Just one bite would be enough to save me
Just one bite would be enough to change me
Just one bite would be enough to fix me

Just one bite was all I needed.
And I would give anything for that one bite
And he knew it. He could see my desperation
And he was not about to let this chance pass
him by

Oh! what I wouldn't give for just one bite
I would trade my promise ring for one of rubber
My crowning glory to be just another number
Just another name on another man's list

As I signed my name out of the book of life

And into his list of ex's, flings, and quick fixes
I had my hero right in the palm of my hand
And all I needed was just one bite

I knew it had to work, I knew it was the remedy
Nothing that costly would be that fake.
After all, I had sold my soul to save my senses
All I needed now was to take one bite.

I only took a bite, but just one bite was enough
I could feel the poison seeping into my system
Already filling my bloodstream with a slow,
painful death.
And this death was the repugnant remedy he
had mis-sold me.

Juice dripping down my chin, I swallow a
mouthful of sin
It's fruit, pleasing to my eyes. It's fruit, good for
food
It's fruit, tasting so sweet in my mouth

As it slowly sinks down my throat and into my
belly

THE SOURCE

Why is my heart heavy?
Why is my soul scorched?
My body longs for the grave
My mind longs for peace

And though I can't explain it
I know in my heart the source of the pain
And it hurts so bad that I want to end it
To end it all completely
I don't have thirteen reasons why
I only have two
One is that you do not love me
And two, I can't stop loving you.

We alone know how much we cry in our closets
Dampened pillows alone bear testament to the
pain within

Only we know what pain lies inside of us
Only we know what song our hearts sing

It is a melody like every other
One that rings with a silent key
As the deafening silence explodes eardrums
I wish, oh I wish...

I just wish he would love me for me.

UNDESERVED GRATIFICATION

Now the length of days grows short
And all the dreams I had are lost.
All the wishes I wish for myself, I wish for you
also.

I pray for joy and peace in my life,
I hope for success
And look forward to a bright future

I am not wishing you this because you are
special
Or because you deserve it,
But because I feel you should get it.

Because I feel you should be rewarded
For all you have done for me -
Nothing!

And for all the times you have made me cry,
Not by your deeds, but by your don't do's
And your ignorant and indifferent disposition
towards me

I just want to say thank you.

WILL NOT BE TAUGHT

Craft, creativity, my hands will learn
To paint and mould, and wield a pen
To express on keys, on drums, on strings
The melody many hearts will sing
My hands will not be taught to hold another's

My arms will not be taught to need another's

My eyes will not be taught to meet another's

My heart will not be taught to love another's

YOU AND ME

Life is too short to wake up with regrets
So love the people who treat you right
Love the ones who don't, just because you can
Believe everything happens for a reason
If you get a second chance, grab it with both
hands
If it changes your life, let it
Kiss slowly. Forgive quickly
God never said life would be easy
He just promised it would be worth it